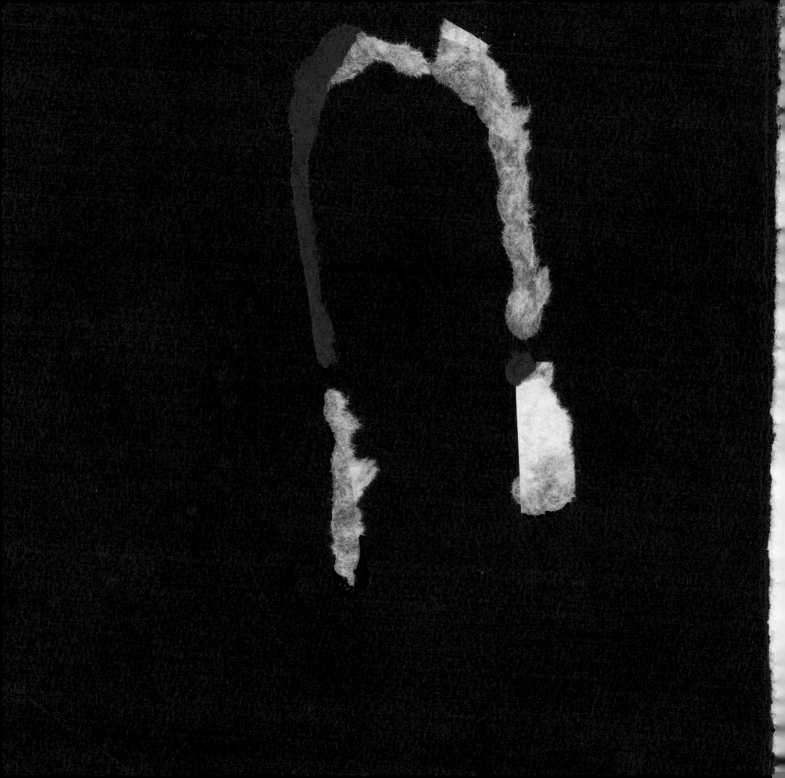

ELEPHANTS

Joe Van Wormer

ELEPHANTS

E. P. DUTTON & CO., INC.   NEW YORK

Library of Congress Cataloging in Publication Data

Van Wormer, Joe   Elephants

SUMMARY: Text and photographs introduce the characteristics
and habits of Asian and African elephants.

1. Elephants—Juvenile literature.   [1. Elephants]   I. Title.
QL737.P98V36   599′.61   75-40323   ISBN 0-525-29210-1

Published simultaneously in Canada by Clarke,
Irwin & Company Limited, Toronto and Vancouver

Designed by Riki Levinson
Printed in the U.S.A.   First Edition
10 9 8 7 6 5 4 3 2 1

To Frank and Madge Ross,
who have nothing in common with elephants
except that they, too, are unforgettable.

A full-grown male African elephant may weigh as much as 14,000 pounds. Some are 11 feet tall. The elephant is the largest and strongest of all four-footed land animals.

There are only two kinds of elephants in the world today: the African elephant (*Loxodonta africana*) and the Asian elephant (*Elephas maximus*). The Asian elephant is a bit smaller than the African (an African male is at left). The Asian is usually no taller than 10 feet and rarely weighs more than 12,000 pounds.

The two kinds of elephants look very much alike, but there are several quite noticeable differences. The African's ears are big—almost too big, it seems (an African female is shown above). The ears cover all of its neck and shoulders and reach down below its chest.

The Asian's ears (a female is above), though still huge by comparison with those of most other animals, are only about one third as large. The lines of their backs are not the same. The female Asian does not have visible tusks.

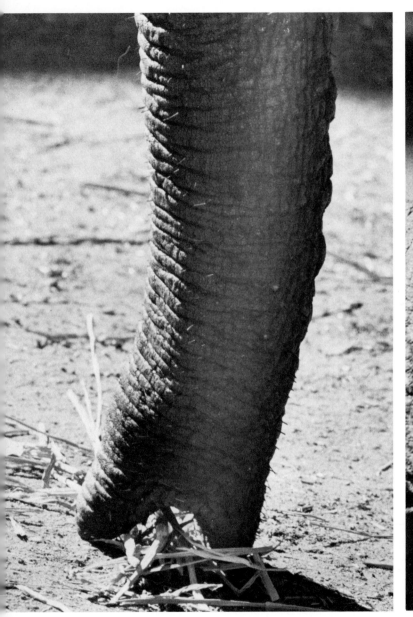

The tip of the trunk shows a marked and easily seen difference. The African elephant (far left) has two small fleshy "fingers" while the Asian has only one.

All elephants are grayish-black in color, but there are variations. The Asian often shows pink and white blotches. Occasionally, a white or albino elephant occurs. In the Tsavo Parks of Kenya, East Africa, visitors are surprised when they see red elephants. They take on this color from the red dust of the country with which they cover themselves.

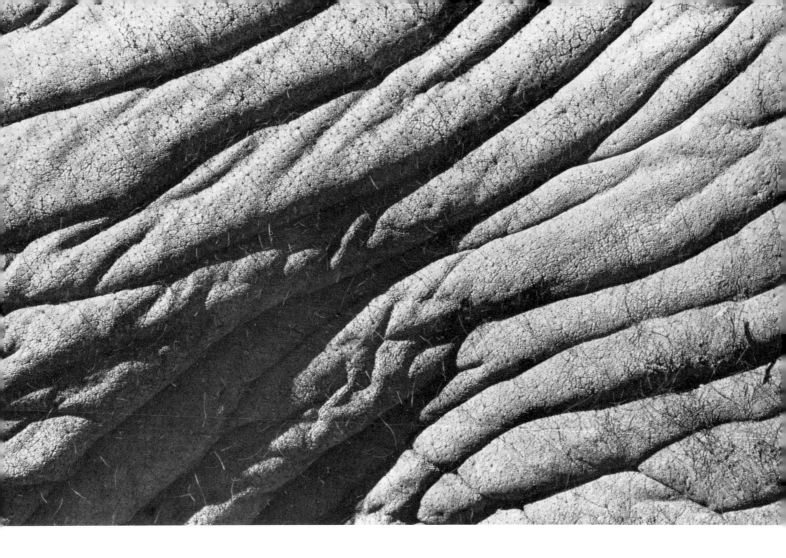

Elephant hide is an inch thick in places but is extremely sensitive, especially to fly and mosquito bites. It wrinkles and sags and bags, especially in the rear, and makes an elephant look as if it was wearing skin a size or two too large. However, this Asian elephant in the San Diego Zoo in California has filled out a bit more than most. Crawling insects find these wrinkles great places to hide and bite.

Unlike so many other mammals, the elephant has nothing to scratch with and must rub the itchy spot against a rock or tree. In these photographs, an itch on the belly, then the trunk, then the backside gets attention.

Full-grown elephants have very little hair except for a noticeable tuft on the end of their tails. This wire-like hair is black and each is about the size of the lead from a lead pencil. Sometimes the hair is lost in family squabbles (as seen above). African natives use elephant hair to make jewelry, which is supposed to bring good luck.

Elephant legs look more like pillars than legs and are designed to carry the animal's great weight. An elephant walks on its toes, which are encased in bag-like skin. The feet flatten out under its body weight and then become smaller when lifted. This enables an elephant to walk through swamps without getting stuck in the mud.

An elephant's feet and legs are all right for holding up its great weight, but the way they are built makes it impossible to run or gallop. About all it can manage is a fast walk. Still, this can seem awfully fast to a person on the ground trying to get out of the way. Elephants have been timed at 24 miles per hour for a short distance. The elephant walks by lifting the front and hind legs on one side at the same time. This gives it a sort of rolling motion even at its normal walking speed of 5 or 6 miles per hour.

One thing an elephant can't do is jump—not even an inch.

An elephant's ivory tusks are actually incisors, or front teeth, in the upper jaw. The tusks of the young African elephant at left are just beginning to show. The largest tusks on record came from an African male. One was 11½ feet long, the other, 11 feet. Together they weighed 293 pounds. About two thirds of the tusks are visible; the other third is embedded in the bone of the skull.

The tusks are mostly used as weapons in fights between bulls, or male elephants, and against enemies. Occasionally they are used for digging for salt, shown here, which elephants like very much, or for water, and sometimes to root out small trees. These tusks grow all during the animal's life. If broken off, they grow back.

Possibly the most remarkable thing about an elephant is its trunk. This is an elongated upper lip which also contains the nostrils. It is made up of flesh and some 40,000 muscles, and acts as a hand and a nose. With it the elephant picks leaves, gathers fruit, crops grass, and throws sand, dust, and water over its body. Through it the elephant screams with rage or squeals with pleasure. The elephant at near right is testing the photographer's scent; at middle right, the elephant's trunk is curled; and at far right, the trunk is relaxed.

The nostrils in the tip of the trunk enable the elephant to determine whether an object is edible or not. By turning the tip in different directions, it can check for the scent of danger or other animals without moving its head, and can smell water 3 miles away.

The small "fingers" on the tips are so sensitive and the touch so delicate that single straws can be easily picked up. Since the trunk is a fairly heavy burden, an elephant may, as the one at right is doing, carry its trunk across its tusks.

Elephants have small eyes set on opposite sides of the head and can see better on either side than straight forward. But they do not really see very well. An elephant relies mostly on its acute hearing and keen sense of smell to find out what is going on nearby.

Wild elephants spend most of their time feeding—about 16 hours a day. A large bull will eat from 300 to 600 pounds of almost any kind of vegetation he can get.

Besides the day-long meal, an elephant needs 30 or 40 gallons of water. During bad dry spells, elephants may travel 20 or 30 miles a day to and from waterholes. When the rivers dry up, they use their sensitive trunks to locate underground water and then dig down to it with their tusks.

The elephant fills its trunk with water (which holds about a gallon and a half), puts it deep into its mouth, and squirts it down its throat. It takes 20 or 30 squirts to satisfy an elephant-sized thirst. This is a noisy, happy occasion.

Elephants do not sleep much. Mostly they take short naps while standing up. Sometimes, however, they lie down and sleep for a couple of hours or so, accompanied by snoring about as loud as you would expect from an elephant.

Family groups are made up of five to fifteen females, or cows, calves, and one or two young bulls. Older bulls generally prefer to be off by themselves. An experienced old cow is in charge of each group.

In Africa, these families often band together into great herds of 200 or more. Individual families can be seen as small groups within the larger herd.

Elephants are naturally peaceable creatures. Their size alone discourages attack. Other large mammals, such as the rhinoceros and hippopotamus, sometimes meet elephants, but they generally ignore each other and go on about their business. Even the larger predators—the lion in Africa and the tiger in Asia—leave the elephant alone. At least they do if they're smart.

An elephant can be very mean when it wants to. With its sharp tusks, a trunk powerful enough to lift a ton of logs, and four gigantic feet, it can dispose of an enemy in any number of unpleasant ways. However, the trunk is not usually used in fighting. When there's trouble, it is kept tucked safely out of the way. Above, a bull charges buffalo feeding at his salt lick. At right, a bull scents out the photographer.

Bulls courting the same cow may have a go at each other with their sharp tusks and, on occasion, serious injury, even death, may result. They fight head to head and try to push each other backward. They may lock trunks and engage in a giant-sized tug-of-war. The object, in either case, is to get the opponent into position where he can be impaled on the other's tusks.

Elephants normally travel in single file and, when they want to, can move along with hardly a sound. Usually, though, their passage is a noisy one accompanied by much breaking of branches, the constant rumble of massive digestive systems busy at work, and the grunts, grumbles, and squeals of casual herd conversation.

Even the largest elephants are surefooted. They approach dangerous slopes and steep ledges cautiously, testing with their forefeet before trusting any doubtful spot with their full weight.

Streams are no obstacle as elephants are good swimmers. However, most African streams are so shallow that the elephant can easily wade across. In some cases where the water is over an elephant's head, it may still wade across with its trunk stuck up through the water and into the air like a submarine's air-gathering snorkel.

Probably no other land mammal enjoys water quite as much as an elephant. On hot days at waterholes they have the time of their lives. Individuals drink, swim, or wallow. They squirt water on themselves, splash about, and trumpet loudly just to show how much fun they're having. They may lie at full length in the water, their expressions showing complete contentment. Small calves run around, chase each other, squeak with excitement, and push each other into the water. They may playfully butt their half-submerged mothers or squirt water on a crusty old bull.

Elephants also take dust baths. They suck up dirt with their trunks and blow it over their bodies. In addition to the pleasurable feel of the fine dust, these baths probably keep some insects away and may relieve the itching of old bites. The photograph at right shows the results of a recent bath of mud, water, and dust.

Elephants are bothered by heat, and, during the hottest part of the day, stand around in the shade and flap their ears more than usual. This cools the blood that flows through their ears and drops body temperature as much as ten degrees.

Elephants also spread their ears when they are angry or about to charge. This makes them look twice as big, which is fearsome, indeed, and may be the reason for it. When one is really mad, it curls its trunk back out of harm's way, turns sideways for a better view, and stands quite still with its tusks raised, prepared for a sudden charge. Now's the time to leave —fast!

Female elephants are ready to mate when 8 to 13 years old; males at around 11 or 12. Individuals may show a special attraction for each other. They stroke one another with their trunks or butt their companions playfully in the ribs. When the mating season finally arrives, the two animals keep constant company. After 60 days or so the female decides to devote herself to approaching motherhood and chases the male away.

Between 19 and 22 months after mating, the calf is born. On rare occasions there may be twins. Shortly before the birth, the expectant mother seeks a secluded spot or some out-of-the-way shelter. Usually, another female, sort of an "aunt," goes along and provides additional protection for the new calf, who is extremely hairy, weighs between 180 and 250 pounds, and is about 3 feet tall at the shoulder.

Within a few minutes the wobbly calf is able to stand, but may lose its balance and take a harmless tumble. Within an hour it is walking and looking for something to eat. Finally it locates one of the two nipples between its mother's front legs. It suckles with its mouth, not the short trunk, which hasn't yet developed into anything more than a nuisance.

The cow constantly watches to see that her calf does not get into trouble. She uses her trunk to care for the youngster, and to let it know she is around looking after things. She may also use it to punish the calf with a good solid whack when it misbehaves.

At the waterhole the smallest calves may not drink at all, but the mothers spray them with their trunks. A calf's first attempts at drinking with its trunk usually result in a lot of bubbles until it learns to suck in rather than blow out. Even then, it is likely to spray water all over its head rather than into its mouth.

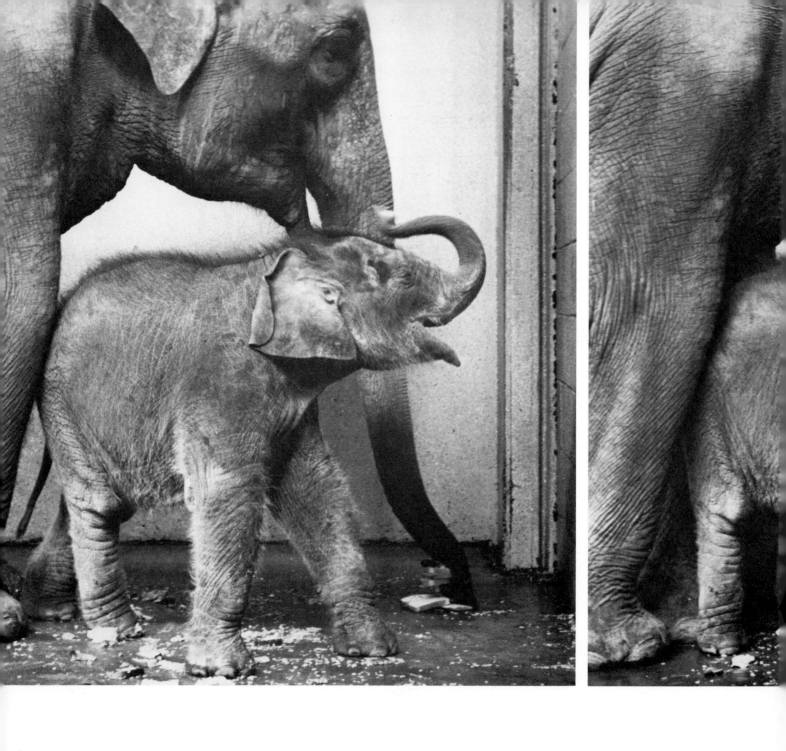

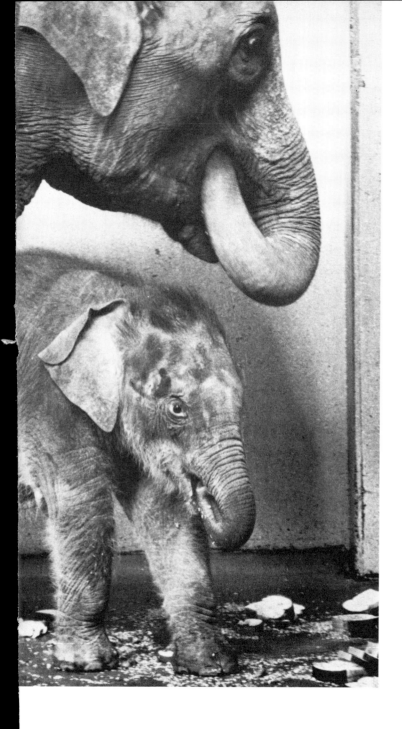

In 1962 an Asian elephant was born in Oregon at the Portland Zoo. This was the first elephant born in the United States in 44 years. The baby was named Packy, short for pachyderm, a name once given to elephants because of their thick skin (*derma*). Like his African kinsman, Packy (shown here) had trouble learning to use his tiny trunk.

A baby elephant needs its mother for food, protection, and companionship. Elephant milk is a special mixture and, without it, an unweaned calf has little chance of survival. Probably just as bad for the calf is loneliness. Fortunately for orphaned youngsters, other cows with calves readily adopt them.

After 3 or 4 months, the baby begins to sample green vegetation. Its mother may hold down a juicy tree branch for the calf to pick at with its tiny trunk. A calf is protected by its mother for up to 10 years, but other calves may be born about every 4 years.

The oldest elephant that ever lived, for which there are records, was an Asian female in an Australian zoo who lived to be 69. But 50 or 60 years is probably closer to an average life span.

Other than man, the chief enemies of this largest of all land animals are the smallest of all land animals—flies, mosquitoes, parasites. Elephants also suffer from indigestion, the common cold, and even mumps.

It is only natural that an animal as large and as unusual as the elephant should be the subject of a lot of interesting and, usually, erroneous stories. Someone started the story that an elephant was afraid of a mouse—the smallest scaring the largest. There's no truth to it. All a mouse could do to an elephant is crawl up its trunk. If this should happen, one good snort would send the hapless mouse soaring through the air.

Elephants are supposed to have amazing memories but it is best to be doubtful when someone insists that an "elephant never forgets." However, trained elephants, which are usually Asian females, do show a remarkable ability to absorb instruction.

Actually, the elephant is such a fascinating animal, it doesn't need any legends or tall tales to make it memorable. Just being what it is, is enough. You can't forget an elephant, and that is no legend.